Soul 2 Soul

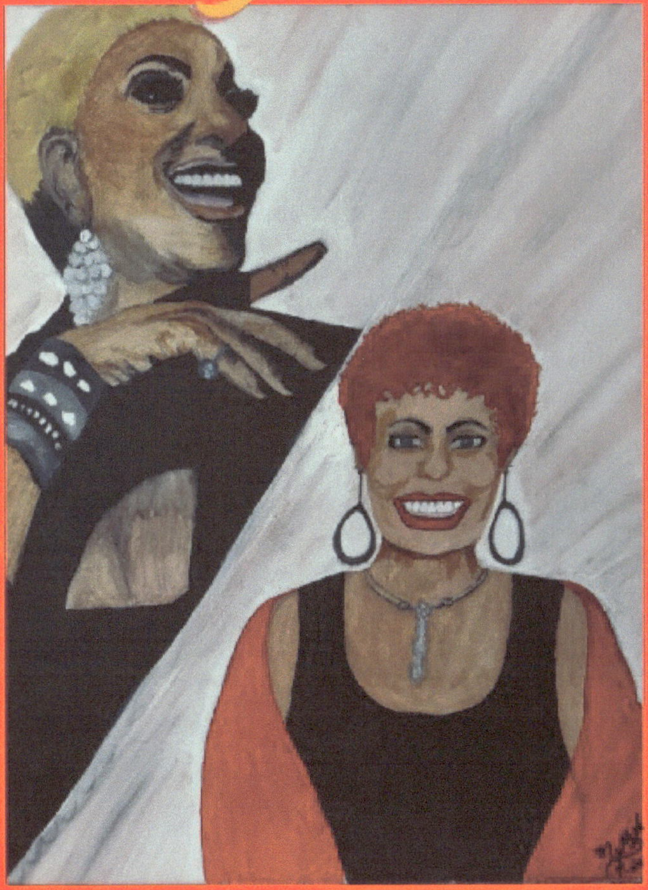

The Goddess of Soul, Martha High
&
Beloved the Soul-Full Poet, Yemaja Jubilee

Copyright © 2021 by Martha High and Yemaja Jubilee

Soul 2 Soul: The Goddess of Soul, Martha High & Beloved the Soul-Full Poet, Yemaja Jubilee

All rights reserved.

Published by KWE Publishing: www.kwepub.com

ISBN (paperback) 978-1-950306-84-8 (ebook) 978-1-950306-85-5

All artwork, including cover, by Martha High.

Layout by Yemaja Jubilee.

First Edition. All rights reserved. No portion of this book may be reproduced, stored in a retrieval system, or transmitted in any form or by any means — including by not limited to electronic, mechanical, digital, photocopy, recording, scanning, blogging or other — except for brief quotations in critical reviews, blogs, or articles, without the prior written permission of the authors.

Soul

2

Soul

The Goddess of Soul, Martha High

&

Beloved, The Soul-Full Poet, Yemaja Jubilee

Contents

Dedication .... i, Yemaja Jubilee

Acknowledgements iii

Foreword .... v, Jenelle Harris

Preface .... vii, Yemaja Jubilee

Introduction .... ix, Yemaja Jubilee

Section One--- Begin with LOVE

To My younger self with Love 3

I get to be 5

I choose Peace 9

Section Two ---Love N Me

Me sits With Me 13

Beloved, Tis safe, I tell you 15

N ME! N ME! 17

Section Three---Christed Heart

Come on Down 23

Down in the Water: The Baptism 25

What a Fellowship 29

Section Four--- Love Outpicturing

All that aging shit!... 35

Got It! Got IT!.. 37

OKAY 39

One More--- Got a fire in my belly And I've gotta tell it!

From an empowered place........................... 45

Afterword.. 51, Martha High

Meet The Authors.. 53

Yemaja Jubilee 53

Martha High 55

Soul 2 Soul Tribe Responses...................... 57

Index of Poems 61

Dedication

To my earthly father, Reverend John H. Brown, who continues to inspire me at 95 years old. And to my two nephews, John Ed Brown, Jr. and Reverend Tyrone Brown, who, along with Daddy, contributed to Section Three of this book.

Acknowledgments

I give thanks to the Source of my Creativity, The Big G (God/Goddess) of this multidimensional Universe, for without it pouring through me there would be no words, rhythm, or rhyme. I embrace the brilliance of this gift that has been bestowed upon me, so I now allow my Soul to overflow through my Poetry.

Thanks to Ms. Brittany Harvin for the use of her image on page 12.

Thanks to Ms. Janine Johnson, of London, England, for the use of her image on page 16.

Thanks to Reverend John Henry Brown for the use of his image on page 20.

Thanks to Kayelily Middleton who has been my friend for over 35 years for her editing skills and her continued support in all areas of my life.

Thanks to Mr. Scott Stewart for his photography skills.

Thanks to Haywood Watkins of Haywood's Hair Images for Hair Design and styling.

Thanks to Haywood's Photo for the photo on page 53.

Thanks to my life partner, L. Roi Boyd III, for his continued support for all my endeavors and listening to my ideas without judgment. Thanks for the encouragement to be the highest version of myself, evolving and continually emerging daily.

Foreword

One morning I went through the mental and emotional transition of letting go of all the negative things around me to allow God to bring positive people and opportunity into my life. I was in the kitchen and gave it all up to God saying "God, it's all up to you." The next day, God worked in my life. I received a text from Beloved asking to interview me. While we spoke, a new energy that I'd never felt before overcame me. A sudden peace washed over me from the top of my head to the tips of my toes.

Beloved is an energy that I like to call "synergy." I am so proud of her and her work inspiring so many people throughout her life and her career. She is an author, co-host, and poet whose work gives so much hope and inspiration. "Breathe Just Breathe" is one of my all-time favorites.

Beloved knows how to move and inspire a crowd; she is a true gem shining bright in the world's crown. When she speaks, light and positivity flow freely. The blazing color of her hair represents the fire that she ignites in each one of us to shine brighter and embrace our true selves. Everyone who encounters her is truly blessed and I am blessed beyond the shadow of a doubt to call this beautiful, inspirational, and passionate woman my family.

One of the most remarkable things about Beloved is the way she handles your soul with kid gloves. But don't be misled by her gentle approach because she isn't afraid to challenge you to step out of your comfort zone to become the best version of yourself. That's why when she calls you "friend," you know you've been inducted into the Queen's dynasty. The royalty of her love is impeccable, and she is the embodiment of what everyone in the world needs as a sister, friend, confidant, and mentor.

Beloved is a soul poet filled with fiery passion, but her impact doesn't stop there. It is an honor to work with her as part of "The Goddess of Soul." Ms. Martha High's team and her work with Cultural Libations paved the way for me to discover another level of love. Her exclusive interview with *Sheen* magazine earned praised from around the globe. It's this impact that sets the stage for Beloved to shine.

It's my greatest honor to call Beloved my dearest friend and mentor. She clears the toxic energy from the room and lets the Big G guide her life and career, which is a lesson to us all. In doing this, she's built her living legacy and made an outstanding impact on each one of us blessed to know her and experience her energy firsthand.

Jenelle Harris
CEO, She Exists

Preface

Many times in my life I have practiced asking Spirit before I fall asleep for the answers and guidance as to how to proceed in my daily living and following its lead in all my affairs. I got this habit from my dad, Reverend John H. Brown. If you asked him something, he would always say "I have to sleep on it and pray on it and then I will give you an answer tomorrow." I had a conversation with Ms. High about writing another book and the possibilities of what she could write about. We were just brainstorming with nothing decided! One night before going to sleep, I asked the Big G for ways to get more of my poetry out in a new way.

On this night, I was in a state of waking and falling back to sleep when an intense feeling of knowing surged through my body. I call this state being "in touch with my creative Genius/Brilliance." I felt the idea in my inner knowingness and heard it with the ear behind the ear, "You are 'Beloved, The Soul-Full Poet' and Martha is 'The Goddess of Soul' plus a visual artist, so combine the two" and *Soul 2 Soul* was born. I was so excited. When I shared the idea with Ms. High, we both agreed to move forward with the idea.

Introduction

I am so immensely proud to have the opportunity to have my poetry interpreted through visual art by the Goddess of Soul, Martha High. I have an appreciation for the soul expressed through her paintings. Her ability to evoke emotion in this medium is engaging and profound. Ms. High is multifaceted and her artistic creations have SOUL, just like all of her music. She always manages to take everything that she desires to do to a "Higher" and deeper level. This is the Soul signature of a multitalented Sister.

To have Soul means "Spiritual--Oneness Used for Living" combined with rhythm and internal flow given by The Big G itself. The poems in this collection were downloaded through my connection with the Divine in various places and at various times. Some early in the morning, some in the rain, others sitting on a log during my forest bathing, and some even inspired by seeing or hearing one word echoing in my Soul or pulling my coattail as my Mother, Marie Harris Brown, would say.

Other times I have been awakened at 2:00 AM and put my pen on the paper and it writes itself. I remember one Friday in mid-August words came pouring though as I was attempting to complete household chores. I had to stop and go sit at my dining room table until it was done because it only comes once. I have learned to either use my telephone to record or put pen to paper. It really is a very spiritual activity and it is always so enjoyable and pleasurable.

According to biblicalstudy.org, 12 symbolizes harmony and peace and is considered a perfect number. There are 12 months in a year, 12 apostles chosen by Jesus, 12 gates to the heavenly city, and 12 tribes of Israel. In numerology it can mean unbridled creativity. In the Unity tradition according to Charles Fillmore, the Divine has given 12 inner powers to all humans. Also, I have attended 12-step programs of all kinds for over 30 years and have healed many past emotional and spiritual scars by working the steps. So, I was led by spirit to choose 12 poems. Now enjoy these 12 Soulful poems that were downloaded to me from the Big G along with the Soulful Art of The Goddess of Soul.

As you read the poems, take a breath, focus on your heart space, put your mind in a contemplative mode and open your awareness to a wider and deeper perspective. This way you will allow the synergy and energy to vibrate in a SOUL-FULL space. Use all songs at the end of each section after Love Notes to enhance and reinforce the effectiveness and positive power of the affirmations..

To My younger self with Love....

A basket full of the colors of the rainbow
That's what came in my heart for you, dear sweet little Black girl today.
'Cause you deserve to be full of joy and gay.
Oh, there now, reach in with your hand guided by The Divine, with your eyes closed to see which color will come your way.
Now do not peek, did you hear what I said...?

Why look what a beautiful soft color--it is *PINK*. ...It is cascading warmth, playfully it soothes your inner most self with love, bringing you joy and nurtures you like a gentle hug from your favorite teddy bear. And cuddling you like your Mother's hug...

OH ! OH! Sweetness, all bright-eyed and your Blackness glowing, and showing, I see you peeking through your fingers, naughty naughty. You no play fair!!

Stop scratching and twisting your hair. Look, you got blue which is a signal for you to trust that though you may be apart from those you love and hold dearly in your heart... You Sweetie are never alone. Just like the Divine painted the sky and the sea *BLUE*. The BIG G--God is always with you...

Hold it I see you have Purple pouring like water though your fingers. Why it is to remind you that you have MAGIC. You are sensitive and with your thoughts you too can wish upon a star, no matter where you are...your Heart's desires are waiting for you, just know that what you are going through ignites a fire of tenacity and courage in you. You will come to see this was meant to be Beloved, so that you can grow graciously and appreciate the prayers of those who love you even more...

Your creativity is blossoming, Baby Girl, because *YELLOW* is whispering softy, please pick me... for this will soon be over... And you can skip merrily down your path to your destiny, happy, joyfully, and FREE......

Hey sweet Black girl, do not forget about me, you cannot have yellow without Green. So, it personifies and harmonize and brings all these colors together... It gives life more abundantly. Smell the freshness in the air and Little Darling of your Mother's Heart...remember to always keep your spark, your shimmer, and your shine. For you are made in Love by love by the Creator of the Universe. So, there is no need to worry. Surround yourself in these colors of the rainbow no matter where you go or how old you become.... always keeping your heart filled with a childlike Spirit... and you will never ever become undone! Do not be mesmerized or hypnotized by all those telling you their version of how you should be...Hold firm and seek Divine Discernment...from the Creator of you and the Universe. And as the years pass by...always dream. Visualize and capture whatever your Soul signature declares. You are expressing your culture using your creativity..., Why I see Orange, and you are transformed by the alchemy of the Magic of the Rainbow's colors flow pouring over you... You, my Beloved Black child, are demonstrating LOVE, LIGHT & Positivity! And so, it is!

I get to be

I get to be, not as you but as me,

I get to breathe, one breath in, one breath out.

I get to see, that each moment is given to me is a gift from the almighty

Yessssss, a precious gift, from thee!

I get to sit in the sweetness of a brand new day called heavenly

I get to witness the inner longings that arise from the depths of my soul

I get to listen to the sounds of ringing, the roaring, and the hunger of knowing

The Source of the One who created me from the imagination of its mind.

And even though Mama carried me in the middle of her belly for 270 days,

I believe it all was meant to be and I get to be free as I choose to be!

I get to live now exploring the inner terrain of this human called YEMAJA, where I dared not have gone before.

In the recess of my Soul there still lies more to uncover and more to me than what the natural eye can see.

I get to say, I can do this earthly adventure not by your rules, but by the guidance of LOVE DIVINE!

I get to play every day to please only me.

Whether walking barefooted in my earth day suit in the wet grass in my yard at 5:00 AM or along the shores of Buckaroe beach, with the sea gulls swirling above my head and a wide brimmed white hat to block out the burning rays of the sun.

I get decide if I am going to hang out with those who do not agree with my inner philosophy, and who are always trying to fix, change and clearly not accept me as me.

HA HA, HAAAAA!

The joke is not on me, 'cause Now I see,

I get to be what I choose, I describe my reality,

My perception is the key coupled with my imagination to being me.

Whatever I desire, whatever I can dream, whatever I can vision, I get to create ME!

I get to BE! I get to be ME!

I get to be

I get to be, not as you but as me,

I get to breathe, one breath in, one breath out.

I get to see, that each moment is given to me is a gift from the almighty

Yessssss, a precious gift, from thee!

I get to sit in the sweetness of a brand new day called heavenly

I get to witness the inner longings that arise from the depths of my soul

I get to listen to the sounds of ringing, the roaring, and the hunger of knowing

The Source of the One who created me from the imagination of its mind.

And even though Mama carried me in the middle of her belly for 270 days,

I believe it all was meant to be and I get to be free as I choose to be!

I get to live now exploring the inner terrain of this human called YEMAJA, where I dared not have gone before.

In the recess of my Soul there still lies more to uncover and more to me than what the natural eye can see.

I get to say, I can do this earthly adventure not by your rules, but by the guidance of LOVE DIVINE!

I get to play every day to please only me.

Whether walking barefooted in my earth day suit in the wet grass in my yard at 5:00 AM or along the shores of Buckaroe beach, with the sea gulls swirling above my head and a wide brimmed white hat to block out the burning rays of the sun.

I get decide if I am going to hang out with those who do not agree with my inner philosophy, and who are always trying to fix, change and clearly not accept me as me.

HA HA, HAAAAA!

The joke is not on me, 'cause Now I see,

I get to be what I choose, I describe my reality,

My perception is the key coupled with my imagination to being me.

Whatever I desire, whatever I can dream, whatever I can vision, I get to create ME!

I get to BE! I get to be ME!

I

choose

Peace

Glorious Grand Rising Beloved.

It's pouring rain but I went outside, and I stood barefooted on the freshly cut grass. It felt so marvelous to allow each wet drop of God's water to cleanse and wash all my worries down into Mother Earth .... Mother Earth, Gia whispered through her vibrations under my feet, Release, Release, my Sweet and allow my energy to give you the gift of Peace.

Choose Peace, Choose Peace...

Allow the mysteries of me to penetrate and saturate your soul. Desperation, Aggravation and Despair are now being replaced with The Big G's Holy synergy of Peace! Peacefulness, Peace just flows through every nook and cranny in your mind, tissue, cell, every muscle. Every bone, every joint. All vital organs dance as they perform their individual tasks guided by the invisible power that created you and all the Glorious Galaxies of the Universe.

You now know.........

Deep in your heart and soul, the Peace you seek is always seeing and seeking you, Sweets...

External circumstances that foster thoughts of fear, doom and uncertainty are just waiting for you to make the choice to bathe them in peace...Those inner places of hurting and disappointments that are lodged in your lower consciousness have risen for your DIVINE purpose to be exchanged for the deepening of The Peace of the Glorious Ever expanding, always present everywhere, all powerful and all-knowing one...

So, focus......

Focus on the truth with the capital T, on your abiding oneness within and without during all adversity...

Which will constantly, if you make the choice, always open the doors. Light your way, open your heart and guide your feelings and all your thoughts to Land of Peace and Serenity!!! And so, it is...!

Affirmation

I am Wonderfully and Marvelously Made!
I am loving, loveable, I am Love!

Love Notes
_____
_____
_____
_____
_____
_____
_____
_____
_____
_____
_____
_____
_____
_____
_____
_____
_____
_____
_____
_____
_____
_____
_____
_____
_____
_____

Song:
"I Love Myself so Much"
by UMA

Section Two

Love N Me

Me Sits with Me

Me sits with me, my Darling Divine Me, to welcome and embrace the inner goddess who wholeheartedly soothes all feelings of uncertainty and distress.

Me sits with me, The Beautiful me, to allow the bathing of my unhealed scars to be set free by something that I can't see, touch, and not detected by my other senses...But Yes, Oh Yessssss, I trust and have faith 'cause I am aware and I know it's there...

Me sits with me, The Sweetheart me, allowing showering drops of Love to penetrating every cell, every tissue, every bone, every joint, every organ and all their functions and even the blood running warmly in my veins ... that makes up me...

Me sits with me, The Bold me, to own my Big Girl Voice and claim my power that was Divinely given to Me by The Big G and not by any human on this earth...

Me sits with me, The Mother me, letting and allowing me to experience the rhythm, the bliss, and the joyful spirit of the child like me.

Me sits with me, The Soulful me, cherishes the lyrics and rhythm embedded in my soul by Love Beauty allowing my uniqueness and creativity to unfold continuously clear for me and for all to see.

Me sits with me, The Brave me, gives me courage and compassion saturated with Angelic heavenly wisdom to inspire, influence and impact humanity.

Me sits with me, The Beautiful me, embraces My inner beauty which is then reflected to me as thee and Us.

Me sits with me. The God part of me that gives me inhalations and exhalation. It breathes me giving me Life, mobility, stability, and agility to keep on moving as I the face all this world's calamity and vulgarity.

Me sits with me, The Badass me, recognizes the multifaceted, multitalented and Magnificent Me that is here to sparkle, shimmer and shine .... Because Me Me is priceless, powerful, and infinite pleasure and possibilities have always been and always will be illuminating just how grateful and glorious My earthly journey continues to be...

Beloved, Tis safe, I tell you

It is safe for you to be who you are
It is safe for you to feel comfortable
In your own skin.

It is safe for you to trust yourself
It is safe to trust your intuition
It is safe to follow your truth...

It is safe to understand and love yourself
It is safe to keep on doing the next right thing
It is safe to hold yourself in high positivity regard...

It is safe to not have all the answers
It is safe to remind yourself that you matter...
It is safe to accept yourself right where you are in this NOW moment

Your Higher Self / The Big G loves and accepts
you unconditionally for you are now
NTUNE, NTOUCH and NSPIRIT

I appreciate the wonderful person that you are and the one you are becoming...

Inspired by "N ME! N ME!"

N ME! N ME!

Today in this now Moment.... I have peace, well-being, brilliance, and most of all LOVE within me!
Laughter resides N ME...
Respect resides N ME...
Joy resides N ME...
Can't you See...It's the REAL ME!!!
Behold Beloved My DIVINE IDENTITY!

Forgiveness resides N ME
Compassion resides N ME...
Peace resides N ME...
Can't you see... It's the REAL ME!
Behold Beloved my DIVINE IDENTITY!!

Well-being resides N ME...
Calm resides N ME...
Zeal resides N ME...
Can't you see... IT'S the REAL ME!!
Behold Beloved my DIVINE IDENTITY!!

Passion resides N ME...
Harmony and Happiness reside N ME
Health and Holiness reside N ME.
Can't you see. It's the REAL ME
Behold Beloved my DIVINE IDENTITY!

Discernment and wisdom reside N ME...
Flow and Faith reside N ME...
Strength and Understanding reside N ME
Can't you see... It's the real me
Behold Beloved my DIVINE IDENTITY!

The BIG G gave all this To Me....'cause N ME, As ME, and Through ME, I get to Be its Magnificent, Victorious, Glorious Tapestry of an energetic, Soulful, Spiritual Being walking and living lovingly with all of Humanity...

Affirmation

I am Wonderfully and Marvelously Made!
Love resides above me, below me, and around me.

Love resides in every part of me and in every ventricle, artery, and every vessel of my beating heart!

Love Notes

_____
_____
_____
_____
_____
_____
_____
_____
_____
_____
_____
_____
_____
_____
_____
_____
_____
_____
_____
_____
_____
_____

Song:
"Pour Yourself in Me"
by Rickie Byars Beckwith

Section Three

Christed Heart

Inspired by "Christed"

Feel it,

Felt it,

God wrote me a letter.

You are beautiful,

You are my beloved.

You are a masterpiece,

Love you like a newborn baby.

Cradle your heart, in a blanket of Love.

Know it.

Show it,

Look, Behold it!

Light in me,

Sees light in you.

You are glowing!

You are out-picturing, outpouring, Divine Brilliance, luminosity, and Love.

Come on Down

Come on down
    Come on down
Come on down the Aisle
    Come on Down
Come on down
    Come on down with a smile!

Preacher preaching Repent! Repent!
Deacon saying Well Well in the corner!
Sisters shouting you can't make me doubt him!

Sit on the Mourners Bench,
    Sit there until you repent,
Sit till you receive a dose of the Holy Ghost!
    Repent of your sins child while you have a chance, Repent with a smile.
Come on Down the aisle,
    Preacher saying Obey thee the Lord.
Deacon praying brothers and sisters you don't want to be lost!
    Sisters shouting Get Saved in Jesus name!

Get up off the Mourners Beach,
Start praising the Savior's Name!
Get up off the Mourners Bench,

And release your anguish and all your pain!

Get up off the Mourners Bench and shouting Hallelujah Hallelujah, I have been saved in Jesus name.

Preacher preaching Your Life will never be the same.

    Deacons saying Amen Amen Amen!

Sisters shouting this old heart of mine been changed...

Now clapping your hands, do a holy Dance!

Speaking in tongues in an inspired trance,

Speaking in tongues that only God can understand!

Uttering Uttering the inherent words of praise that glorify Almighty God that sits high and looks low.

Preacher preaching The Holy Ghost is in here

    So, let us all stand!

Deacon clapping their hands and stomping their feet on the one beat

    Sisters shouting Lord, Lord, once again the Devil has lost his bet!

Extend your hands in the Air into God's care

crying and weeping

You feel your moment of truth

filled with joy you have landed in the

Peace that all your life you sought!

Preacher preaching, thank you God another soul has been saved,

    Deacon saying, Amen Amen Amen!

Sisters shouting, You can't make me Doubt him!

Down in the Water: The Baptism

Take me to the Water
    Take me to the Water
        Take me to the Water
            Baptize Me!

Down in the water
    Down in the water
        Down in the water my body must go
            Submerge me, purge me, Baptize me
                Allow my soul to flow flow and let all my sins
                be washed away so I can grow!

A rite of passage to show that I now accept Jesus Christ as my Lord and Savior

I have a changed mind and an attitude of Gratitude for what led me to repent

I am highly blessed and highly favored

No longer do I carry the burdens of guilty and dirty rotten shame

Y'all, I do declare, I have been saved by his blood and in his name!

I now die a righteous death, the death of my old self.

No more cussing, drinking, drugging or always saying you are to blame...

As I allow my tongue to take the Lord's name in vain.

No stinking thinking, but a parting of my ways not to be like what I was before...

Before my Savior gave me a new name,

You see I now have a new name, a new name

I let go of all my selfishness and that low-down dirty shame.

Rev. Lackado, what say you?

Child of God today you will be made brand new,

Like John the The Baptist who Baptized Jesus the Christ

Upon your faith and the confession of your sins

I now Baptize you!

In the name of the Father, The Son, and the Holy Ghost

Come up out of the Water with a fire in your belly cause God has now empowered you!

No bells and whistles nor claim to fame,

    But now let us all proclaim.

        A new creature in Christ,

           Who can now maintain

                And tell the story with high praise

                    I got a new name over in glory!

                        A new home in the heaven
                            surrounded by 12 archangels
                            and the son of God's love.

The cool cool water my body went down in it,

    I have been submerged, purged, and Baptized

That set my soul free!

    So now I am filled with light and I now glow

One thing I know for sure,

    To hell I won't go.

Right Hand of Fellowship, What a Fellowship

&

Give Me That Old Time Religion

Come gather around

Get up off and out of them pews

And come on down

Come many and not just a few

The energy and synergy of the Holy Ghost

Is presently here and flowing through everybody and that means you my dear, you in the corner and all you Sisters and Brothers too.

Extend your right hand as this soul extends their right hand to you

Now let's Raise a hymn as you sing

'Cause this, my Brothers and Sisters, is the gospel truth. It's truly GOD's Thing

"Amazing Grace, how sweet the sound

That saved a wretch like me, I once was lost but now I am found, was blind but now I see"

Now I will have a closer walk with thee

Welcome to the fold

In Spirit and in truth

You have now pledged your self

To the king of king and Lord of Lord

Now allow him to guide you

Release all your struggles

'Cause he now is driving your car

And he can maneuver better than you

he will clear the way and see you through

Toils and snares will come a looking for you

But that's no problem

'Cause you have been made brand new

This is no game, no game I said

For you have been converted

So you no longer must worry

Or rush around like mice in maze and in a hurry

I got a new name

And I am not ashamed

'Cause I have been saved by the blood and washed in Jesus' Name

I got a new walk and a new talk

For God has changed this old heart of mine

I have peace in my mind body and soul

'Cause Jesus the Christ has made me whole

His light in me is brilliant and bright and better than the White House Christmas tree

And I now shine like the morning star

I know I have religion and I am no longer insane 'cause I been saved, and Baptized in My Savior's name...

Affirmation

I am Wonderfully and Marvelously Made!

I am no longer bound by my old thoughts, patterns of behaviors that do not glorify, and personify the love of The Big G in myself and others. I am Free in Spirit, mind, and body!!

Love Notes

_____
_____
_____
_____
_____
_____
_____
_____
_____
_____
_____
_____
_____
_____
_____
_____
_____
_____
_____
_____

Song: "I Have Something to Shout About"
by Martha High

Song:
"Jesus is Love"
by Lionel Richie & The Commodores

Section Four

Love Outpicturing

All that aging shit!

The older I get, the younger I become,

Cause no one gets to tell this SISTAR,

How aging is supposed to be done.

Yes, my hair is fire engine red

And my lips are green or purple at times.

I am unique, Bold, & Black! I am a Queen! I exude The Big G's divine light and Luminosity for all the world to behold. Snap! Snap! Here what I say...I am one of a kind, and I will not allow you to mess with my mind!

You see age is but a number that does not have to define you or me.

Why it is simply crazy when you follow the rules of normalcy,

I do know for sure that if you do not move every day in some way there will be a time you desire to move, and your mind says yes and your body says hell no, sugar plum ... We ain't moving today!

Yes, I can see this for myself 'cause all that you say means nothing to me.

You are not me, nor will I allow you to determine my reality and define my destiny.

I will defy those odds you see, because I am the Beloved of the BIG G and It tells me that what I think about I bring about.

I will not hang around those who complain, moan, and tell their stories repeatedly of misery and pain.

On my path, my journey on this earthly plane I get to do it my way. I accept who I am, where I am, with radical self-acceptance without divine discontent.

So out the front door of my mind, between the neurons and synapses

There are no memory lapses...

Just a tender, gentle voice, in my Soul sanctuary in a whisper.

I hear it say...

No, you didn't come here to stay.

But my Beloved one, you can and you will flourish, bloom, and grow from the inside out in a wholesome, vigorous, and dynamic way...and AGE and aging are just a word! Grounded in Spirit You get to do your life... ... YOUR WAY.

I did it my way!!!

Got It! Got IT!

I have become unified, and Today at this present moment, right now moment, I am not mystified, nor am I mesmerized, Child, I sure ain't sanitized! Got it! Yes, Yes, I am holy sanctified in the energy of The BIG G – my 40 trillion cells vibrate because they begin to dance not to the music of the Fifth dimension, but they are already in the Fifth dimension of oneness, wholeness and Love. Goodness Gracious, I am believing, I am receiving 'cause The Big G knows what I Be needing... What I be needing!!

Believing is not some game I play, What I say, What I say! No Game That I play... No Game that I play! Gurl, I be getting weary, worn, and fray.

No question need be asked, but my curiosity just wants to allow my mind to stray. Allowing, Allowing, Letting, Letting the Big G have its way is the answer to my inner dilemma, turmoil, and distress... Lordy, Oh Lord, no need to let this 3-D thinking be, no need to reside there, to living from my head...the lies, the voices constant chatter, an inner roommate taking up space in my thinking. No need to wrestle, toss and turn, be at war with myself like nobody is home inside my head...saying

Living small minded, living with lack and limitation, living like a zombie, parading around in the Walking dead zone...Hey Girl. is anybody home? Existing, my God, this is a distraction placed in my mind by the enemy, 'cause not believing was taught to me by people and systems who swore that they had my best interest at heart. But they too drank the Kool-Aid just like our ancestors before them. Grounded in someone else's concept of The Big G and having a white image as the god of their understanding. A Christed heart, A Christed heart gives you strength and you come to know living without believing sure can be deceiving! Lord have mercy, all the lies that I have been told!

Believe in what you say, what you say! Why just look around you Beloved one. I can hear Granny Mae's voice in my head, as she stands in the kitchen with her hands in the pockets of her yellow and green cooking apron with her head cocked to the side, "Honey Child, do not dare let anyone, be they black or white red or brown, shake a finger in your face, yell at you to compel you, or sweet talk you in to selling your soul, deterring you from the flow of your innate goodness which makes you stray from the path of the Divine.

Wake up! Wake up! Open your eyes and see with the eye behind the eye and hear with the ear behind the ear so that you get an inner standing in your heart, 'cause from the Divine all good things flow.

It is the Big G who makes your life outstanding and not demanding. Believe. Believe and you shall receive, receive what you have been seeking after.

Breathe, Breathe Breathe

Now hear the soft whispers of your messages, allow the wind to kiss you, as it cradles your face in it hands. Listen...Pray and trust and allow your faith no matter how small, help you visualize, actualize, and materialize your heart's desires.

So, my child Beloved, Beloved,

Pretty please, please Beloved!

OKAY

A victim

no longer I will Be!

Okay! It's okay if you do not like me 'cause baby I got what it takes, and I declare I actually not only like myself...I adore what I see and feel in the mirror looking back at me...even embrace and bless my stark-naked body in floor length mirror...I love the Black skin that I reside in...Yeah Yeah!

Okay! It's okay that you don't accept me, because dear one, your non-acceptance will not rattle me or make me become undone. You see I am grounded, centered, and forced in the Almighty Divine one.

Okay! It's okay that you don't respect me, neglect me, because precious one ...I do.

I hold myself in High positive regard no matter what you say and treat myself like I am the best thing since sliced bread with honey on the top and a hot white chocolate mocha from Starbucks on the side! You bet I do!

Okay! It's okay that you think I am crazy and going to hell...Boy oh Boy are you in for an overwhelming surprise that will blow your damn peace of mind--a rude awakening to say the least...to know crazy you must be crazy 'cause like I have been told, you spot it, you got it.

Now Run tell that.

You see what you think and say no longer matters to me. It does not make you right and me wrong.

'Cause in Love of the Divine, I have been Defined... I always have been and will always be an Amazing Awesome Woman continuously emerging, evolving, shining, and shouting it on the world's stage. That's Truth with a capital T. And pure Agape love orders my steps in every moment of the day...practicing spiritual principles in all my affairs. And victoriously yes, wearing my red hair--just look at them all stare!! A victim I will no longer Be!!!

Affirmation

I am Wonderfully and Marvelously Made!

I love and accept my Magnificence; I am a Masterpiece!

Love Notes

_____
_____
_____
_____
_____
_____
_____
_____
_____
_____
_____
_____
_____
_____
_____
_____
_____
_____
_____
_____
_____
_____
_____
_____
_____
_____

Song:
"Greatest Love of All"
by Whitney Houston

One More

Got a fire in my belly

And I've gotta tell it!

From an empowered place

No need to crawl, walk, March to the rhythm of your drum, 'cause Baby I got what it takes. I am Dancing, skipping, merrily, and Cheerfully in the flow of Spirit care and Grace...

No longer shy, unassuming, docile, or keeping silent as I live a ho hum life...bored stuck and rigid...all covered by my own shit...blaming you for dumping your shit on Me and creating my misery...

Got a fire N my Belly... I got to tell it!

I AM living from an empowered place!

No longer do I lie, deceive, cheat or undermine or manipulate those who I perceive are less than me because of a caste system that was set up to annihilate, keep us in our place so they could feel superior because of the Blackness of my skin and not a member of this Human race.

No longer do I listen to what the news says, be it Fox, CNN, CBS, NBC or MSNBC, The White House rhetoric or the Tweet from a being who really is fulfilling his purpose by dispensing negativity and his own narcissistic way of thinking and living ..

GOT a FIRE N MY BELLY and I got to tell it...

I'm Living from an Empowered Place!

No longer listen to he say, She say or they say or those who pass along gossip or criticize to defame, destroy, or defeat others....Gotta watch them 'cause what they say about them they will surely reap and what they say is really a reflection of how they see themselves that comes out of their mouths as they speak!

No longer am I bound to being the best fuck in town 'cause I had to sleep around to push down all the pain of not loving myself and I just settle for the crumbs from any man's table.

Got a Fire N My Belly, I got to tell it...

I'm living from an Empowered place!

No longer must I marry Tom, Dick, or Harry to give me a name, or fix, change, or their emotional unavailability or neediness is their only claim and once again I become insane...

No longer do I choose to suffer or be a martyr or poster child for not-enough-ness...unworthiness, spineless, purposeless being with a fragile ego who sells their soul to the highest bidder for a millimeter of second to validate my whole existence...

Got a fire N my Belly & I got to tell it...

I'm living from an Empowered Place

No longer will I be held back and bound by generational patterns of anger, rage, drugging, drinking, eating, workaholic or religiosity and money to cover up and be embedded by all that generational pain and truck loads of shame, shame...

No longer! No longer! No Longer!

Cause I got a fire N my Belly....& I got to tell it!

Brilliant, Bodacious, Beautiful,

Spiritual, Sassy, Sexy and Soulful

Boy oh Boy I just said a mouthful

No need to be Doubtful

Cause I am a Bold Badass Soul

I now realize that I am the gift that

I bring to the world and I wield my power and uniqueness and on purpose as I continue

to unfold...

I now live from an Empowered Place!!

Now Run tell it... 'Cause you been told!

Affirmation

I am Wonderfully and Marvelously Made!
I smile, I sparkle, I shimmer, I sizzle, and I shine!

Love Notes

_____
_____
_____
_____
_____
_____
_____
_____
_____
_____
_____
_____
_____
_____
_____
_____
_____
_____
_____
_____
_____
_____
_____
_____
_____
_____
_____
_____
_____

Song:
"Shining Star"
by Earth, Wind & Fire

This is not the end

It was amazing to have you come on this journey as I invited you to see and feel what is revealed by my Soul though my poetry. I consider all the poems gifts from my Higher power, The Big G. I downloaded each one of these poems. One day three were given and then eight poems in one week. I just sat down with my pen and paper and accepted them as gifts that I was to share with you in this book at this time.

My desire for you is that you will live your life with SOUL each moment of your days. SOUL- Spiritual Oneness Used for Living. My oneness with the Divine allows me to be... Beloved, The Soul-Full Poet, a Sassy Soulful Badass Woman.

Afterword

What an experience this has been!

I'm gonna explain my feelings when this "Nubian Queen" (Yemaja Jubilee) inspired me to express my feelings by creating paintings from the poetry she had written!

I agreed to do six paintings and the cover. I had no idea how, where or what, I would come up with until I got started!

Once I read the first two poems you had written, Yemaja, I was in awe! I said, "OMG! She's truly blessed with words!" The poems made me feel like they were beyond my imagination and expectations! So, I read them again and I thought "yes, just as I thought, from the beginning, they are indeed powerful and inspirational!" I felt the spirit come over me saying, "not to worry, you can do it, take your time, listen, seek, THE BIG G's got you!"

Honestly... an amazing 3 months was put into this work but less than usual. Why less time? I was excited, nervous, happy and I did not want the adrenaline in my head to stop! Wow! I normally spend months creating a painting, but I knew my time was limited, plus I wanted to do my best ever, so I prayed and kept praying and of course, the "Big G" answered my prayers—"if you know me, you should trust me...surely, I will guide you!"

I read every one of her poems with the understanding that her poems are rooted deeply from within her heart and soul which enabled me to express through my paintings what I felt, what her heart & soul were saying and giving.

These poems are guidelines for love, strength, harmony, and mostly who you are and can be, to accept where you come from, how to be strong in seeking God's love. Accepting Him as your confidante and Him only to guide you! To find your inner peace with God! To stand strong no matter what color, no matter what race! Concernment...and never doubt or forget the "Big G" made you! Be at peace. Love yourself. Know your blessings!

Christed is the love of life and happens when you follow the "Big G." Your light will shine through others when you guide them to love, to be kind to one another, to teach them to pray, teach them the Bible, teach them the path of righteousness--to give God all the praise because we're all as one under the sun.

Thank you, my Nubian Queen Sista! This has been the most exciting and first time of creating artwork for such a grand project *Soul 2 Soul*! Such an awesome idea!

I'm very honored to be the one you chose to do this exciting & meaningful book of Poetry & Arts!

May you be blessed with many years to follow!

Sincerely,
Much Love always,
Martha High

Meet the Authors

Yemaja Jubilee

Yemaja Jubilee is Co-Founding Director of *Cultural Libations,* an inspirational speaker, poet, author, & song writer. She is a member of the Core Management team of *StudioW Buzz* and Creative Consultant. She serves as *Community Liaison* for Martha High, The Goddess of Soul, and is currently the Co-Host for *"It's High Time"* and *"The Boomerang"* shows, both featured on *StudioW Buzz*. She hosts the *"Love, Light & Positivity"* show on Josi's Inspirational Network. She has served as co-host on *"At The Table with Ms. B"* & *"Bring Who You Are."*

Ms. Jubilee has thrived during the current global crisis and has been featured in *Sheen, MTM, Lemonade Mindset* and *On Purpose Woman* magazines, and she has graced the cover of *Nish* Global Magazine. She also serves as a contributing writer for *On Purpose Women* and guest columnist for the *Charlotte Gazette* where she is writing about her childhood experiences, entitled "Growing up Black N Charlotte County."

Her extraordinarily successful poetry book, *Couldn't Keep It To Myself,* was released 2017, and is available on Amazon. Yemaja is working on her next book, *Sisters Sitting N the Blessing,* scheduled to be released in early 2021.

With over 10 years as a TV/radio hostess, Yemaja's guests have always been luminaries in their various fields as they continue to bring to the world the highest and best version of themselves. Her interviews are geared specifically to what her audience needs to know about her guests in their area of expertise with a very personal touch. With a positive and joyful Spirit, her listeners are inspired, influenced, and encouraged to believe in possibilities and that there is no box. She has earned accolades for her moxie and transparency while encouraging others to be authentic and express their uniqueness in her delivery of inspirational speeches. Her soulful poetry continues to be in high demand in many different arenas from conferences, jazz shows, to virtual platforms and Spiritual platforms where she delivers "Spoken words."

Yemaja's latest endeavor, *Celebrity Buzz* on studiowbuzz.com, showcases the artistry and accomplishments of some of our favorite celebrities. You will be entertained in a whole new way by introducing you to their journey to stardom, their triumphs, and how they utilize their gifts. Join Yemaja on the 2nd and 4th Thursdays of each month at 6:00 PM EST for these amazing stories with your favorite celebrities!

Contact Yemaja @ landnluv117@gmail.com for inspirational speaking and Creating "Special" Personalized Celebratory Poems and Greeting Cards.

Martha High

Named Martha High by James Brown, the Godfather of Soul, Martha Harvin launched her singing career in the mid-1960s with The Jewels. Brown saw High and The Jewels perform at the famous Apollo Theater in New York and invited them to join him on the road with the James Brown Review. Martha spent the next 32 years with Brown and became the longest-performing artist with the Review.

Amid her success with Brown, Martha joined other legendary artists on stage including Michael Jackson, Bo Diddley, BB King, and Maceo Parker. She was featured in *The Blues Brothers* film and the television series, *New York Undercover*.

Martha is a true diva in today's music scene and is one of the most accomplished soul and blues singers in the industry. With her career now spanning five decades, Martha is a highly sought-after performer. After working with Maceo Parker and his band for 16 years, Martha currently enjoys a successful solo career.

She's performed for audiences around the world in addition to giving special guest performances on over 50 television series featuring talented hosts like Johnny Carson, Jay Leno, David Letterman, Arsenio Hall, Jerry Springer, and Jonathan Ross. She's also one of the best live performers in the business and has taken the stage at the Montreal Jazz Festival, the Indianapolis Jazz Festival, and many other live events throughout Europe and Japan.

Contact Martha @hiomrod@juno.com for inspirational speaking and scheduling appearances.

Discography

- Martha High
- Live at The Quai Du Paris
- Martha High with the Shaolin Temple Defenders
- Soul Overdue with UK's Speedometer
- It's High Time

Published Works

- *He's a Funny Cat, Ms. High: My 32 Years Singing with Mr. James Brown* An intimate look into Martha's life, career, and her time on the road with James Brown, *He's a Funny Cat* is candid and heartfelt as Martha openly shares her experiences, a few never-told-before stories, and what Brown meant to her as a boss, mentor, brother, and friend.

Awards

- Jus Blues Denise LaSalle Recording of Excellence Lifetime Award

Videos, Performances, and Interviews

- Martha High YouTube

SOUL 2 SOUL TRIBE COMMENTS

Soul 2 Soul is a poetic journey led by Yemaja Jubilee and Miss Martha High into the human experience, self-awareness, womanhood, sisterhood, fellowship, and spirituality. Reading this collection was like having a calming and loving conversation with a trusted friend. Each passage serves as a fog cutter during troubled times where many forces compete for our attention, especially for many of us who seek truth and direction. A highly recommended read by two visionary creators of poetry and art.

Michael Edell
San Francisco Bay Area, California

This is a fun and inspirational book of poems! Yemaja and I have known each other over 30 years and I have always loved how she can go deep inside and bring forth words of wisdom and enthusiasm for life. Life for all of us is a series of lessons presented by the Universe (the big G) like stepping-stones leading us deeper and deeper into the discovery and true nature of our authentic selves if we are brave enough to do it. Yemaja is a true example of learning the lessons and moving along the path of life and illustrating it with her poems! And the illustrations by Martha High are fabulous accompaniments.

Rev. Kayelily Middleton
Raleigh, North Carolina

I read your many words and they are raw and cathartic to the soul. Your willingness to be vulnerable yet unapologetic for speaking the truth as YOU! is exhilarating. "All that aging shit" resonates with me, life is not calculated or measured in matter, place, time, or space. We came to play on and on ~ ain't that some cosmic sh*t.

Rev. Georgia Johnson
Richmond, Virginia

Authentic! Exciting! Heartfelt! First of all, Yemaja, you spoke of colors in Section One, "to my younger self with love," after I was mesmerized by such brilliant colors on the front cover with your portrait and that of Martha High, Visual Artist. The concept of her individual paintings befitting each poem is nothing less than masterful!

Reading your poetry, I could hear your voice, and instantly it became the voice of a thousand women shouting, "Amen!" I could picture the sisterhood celebrating our rebirth, a vision of us measuring the beating, the beating of our hearts, that we may, indeed, as you stated, "...focus on our heart space."

Sylvia Harvin
California

This author captures the essence of emotions and thoughts in her delivery of lines for Soul renewal and review. "Beloved, Tis Safe, I tell You" speaks to the heart in to remind where "Safe" lies. Speaking to one's higher self to comfort and to secure the internal waves.

Sheila Richardson
Richmond, Virginia

I needed *Soul 2 Soul* in this time of so much chaos, hurt and distrust. Jenelle Harris writes in her foreword in this book of asking God to bring positive people and opportunity into her life and that is who Yemaja is. She is that to those who know her. This book of poetry touches so many facets of my life reminding me of who and what I aspire to be. Poems that express that it is alright to just be and to see the inner God that is ever present in my life. These poems and affirmations are like calming water to the soul that also lets me shout with certainty "a victim no longer I will be." Thank you, Beloved, for letting me be a part of this.

Penelope Anthony
Richmond, Virginia

One of my favorite poems "Come on down" resonates with me because it captures some of my fondest childhood memories. You have a finesse with your writing, and it paints a vivid picture of that moment. It's amazing how our childhood memories reflect to be one in the same, although we have never discussed it. Thank you for taking me back to a happier place in my life and reflect on the time that was spent with my darling (or dear) Grandmother, Marie.

Cozzette Dushon Brown-Abrams
Richmond, Virginia

I am inspired by your work. Your heart-inspired poetry, inspired heart-centered commentary. I am honored to be able to comment on this amazing poetry from the heart. As I read it, I saw girls and women of all ages seeing themselves in the beloved, in the experience of nature, and in the rainbow of color that lives in every soul.

It is truly a Divine experience to walk through this poetry. It takes you straight to the heart of Spirit in a healing and self-assuring way. I also like that there are journaling pages for sharing what is in the heart of the reader. I really like the soul's journey of forgetting and awakening in Section 4, and I love your Granny!

Yemaja-you are the rainbow, and you share your gift of color and soul with all women-and the feminine energy in every soul! Your journey is truly a soul's journey for all of us!

Rev. Laura Bennette
Richmond, Virginia

Precious Yemaja Jubilee, I love your poetry! It sings, and it's the rhythm of joy. It is life-affirming, hope giving, and strength proclaiming! May God bless You!

Judith Bentley
Richmond, Virginia

These are some of the most powerful assortment of words I have ever read. You truly have an eclectic way of expressing the power of God and your gratitude for the Supreme being. I could not help but come alive in my own journey as I could relate to your ability to conquer your fears and insecurities.

Transformation took place right before my eyes as your words painted the canvas of my imagination of who you really are--a beautiful soul, full of God's grace and mercy. You are light!

Tracey R Kincaide
Chicago, Illinois

I was elated and grateful to read all your poems. You have a natural touch with poetry. They are all so soulful and personal, I cannot choose just one. However, "I Choose Peace" rocks through my veins! I love outdoors and "Mother Earth". There I can release all of me, with no inhibitions, no grudges, and no malice. Just pure soulful inner peace. The other is "Empowered." I speak my mind! I am Empowered! I am now choosing to live in an Empowered Place!

Lois Campbell
New York, New York

INDEX OF POEMS

All that aging shit! 35

Beloved, Tis safe, I tell you 15

Come on Down 23

Down in the Water: The Baptism 25

From an empowered place 45

Got It! Got IT! 37

I choose Peace 9

I get to be 5

Me sits With Me 13

N ME! N ME! 17

OKAY 39

To My younger self with Love 3

What a Fellowship 29

www.ingramcontent.com/pod-product-compliance
Lightning Source LLC
Chambersburg PA
CBHW040355190426
43201CB00039B/31